GHOST

FRIGHTENING ENCOUNTERS

VOLUME 3

Compiled and edited by
Tom Lyons

GHOST FRIGHTENING ENCOUNTERS: VOLUME 3

Copyright © 2020 Tom Lyons

All rights reserved. No part of this may be reproduced in any form without the author's prior consent, except brief quotes used in reviews.

All information and opinions expressed in *Ghost Frightening Encounters: Volume 3* are based upon personal perspectives and experiences of those who were generous enough to submit them. Tom Lyons does not purport the information presented in this book is based on accurate, current, or valid scientific knowledge.

Acknowledgments

It's certainly no easy task for people to discuss their encounters with the paranormal. I'd like to personally thank the many good people out there who took the time and energy to put their experiences into writing.

To respect those who were involved, some of the names have been altered or replaced with the word "anonymous".

Would you like to see your report in an issue of *Ghost Frightening Encounters*?

If so, all you have to do is type up a summary of your experience, and email it to Tom Lyons at:

Living.Among.Bigfoot@gmail.com

Contents

Report #1 1

Report #2 10

Report #3 18

Report #4 37

Report #5 48

Report #6 61

Report #7 69

Report #8 (Steve Molloy's Report Continued) .. 81

Conclusion 89

Editor's Note 91

Mailing List Sign Up Form 93

Social Media 95

About the Editor 97

GHOST FRIGHTENING ENCOUNTERS: VOLUME 3

Report #1

I was a sophomore in high school when my telecommunications class received an assignment where we had to pick a product and create a fake commercial. I worked with two of my classmates, Cam and Julian, and we all agreed to make a commercial for Vanilla Coke. We must've chosen that product because this was back in the 90s and it had just recently hit the market.

While we were looking for a place to shoot the commercial, Julian mentioned an old garage separated from the house his family just moved to. He explained how it had an attic that would be perfect if we wanted to create something with a horror theme. Ultimately, we agreed that we should give it the look of a horror movie that had a comical twist.

When Cam and I went over to the house that weekend, I remember being a bit worried whether one of us would fall through the floorboards. It was immediately evident that Julian hadn't spent much time scoping the place out because he even seemed unsure of where he should walk. The place was super dark and dusty, and the floorboards creaked with every step we took. It was a pretty spacious attic, and it even contained two or three smaller rooms that were probably intended for a bathroom and extra storage spaces. While we were reviewing our storyboard, we heard something coming from one of those smaller rooms. It sounded like someone had been hiding and then stood up quickly to run away. That made no sense because there wasn't anywhere to escape to aside from the staircase near us.

After the noise settled, Cam started giving Julian a hard time, telling him he was too "chicken shit" to go check things out in his own home. Well, Julian took the challenge and headed in that direction with a flashlight in hand. I remember how Cam and I were amid a discussion about something completely unrelated when we were interrupted by Julian's scream. Not only did something frighten him, but it also sounded like he tripped when running back in our direction.

"Dude, you alright?" I shouted from across the extensive attic. I could make out a cloud of dust that was lightly illuminated by the flashlight. It was as our friend was standing up that the accident happened. The floorboards gave out, and we heard Julian let out another yelp as he plummeted to the first floor.

"Oh shit!" Cam yelled as he went racing down the steps. Without delay, I headed toward the area where it sounded like Julian went through the floor. I arrived at the location, prompting me to keep my distance. Still, I was close enough to where I could see the first floor. Fortunately, Julian had fallen onto what looked like boxes of old clothes. He was a little banged up, but we were just glad to see he was still conscious.

When he looked up and saw me, he began shouting at me to get out of there. Initially, I thought he was referring to the weak floor because he didn't want me to fall. But then he said the words, "there's someone else up there!"

"Huh?" I said, assuming he was confused. But it was as soon as I shined the flashlight toward one of the storage spaces that I saw the woman. She was hanging from the ceiling by a rope that was tied around her neck. Her long red hair covered most of her face, but I could see enough of her eyes to see that she was somehow aware of me. Soon, she wrapped her hands around the noose and began tugging like she was desperate to get out of it. I didn't know what else to do other than run toward her and try to set her free. It all happened so fast I wasn't able to think clearly.

It was when I got within a few feet of her that she snarled at me, sort of like the way an animal would act when feeling threatened. I jumped backward and immediately withdrew my hands that were already on their way toward the woman's throat. As fast as I could, I ran out of that storage room and toward the staircase. I was so frightened that I didn't even consider how I could have fallen through the floor on my way to the stairs.

Julian's mother was home and must have heard the commotion because she was outside when I had gotten downstairs and rendezvoused with the others. Julian was amid explaining that there was a woman upstairs that he had never seen before. His mom called the police to come to check things out, and I wasn't surprised to learn that they didn't find anyone up there. They seemed far more concerned by the fact that a kid had just fallen through the floor. Frankly, I didn't have a whole lot of input for Julian's mother or the cops; it seemed sort of futile to try to convince them about what I saw. The amazing thing was how my friend's description aligned perfectly with what I saw. What was that woman doing hanging up there?

As far as I know, Julian never did any significant research on the history of the property. Still, I got the impression that he wanted to avoid learning anything much about it. And Even if his mother knew some things, she didn't offer up any of the information. I doubt she believed the details about the hanging lady, but I think they lived in that place for quite a few years after the event, so I imagine they had to have seen something at some point.

I have never seen anything else like that since that day. Given the number of reports on them, it makes me wonder why they're not a more socially acceptable topic of discussion. Why is it that there are certain things out there that have been labeled as taboo? As crazy as it might sound, I can't help but feel like that was influenced by people who wanted to deter people from the truth. Maybe I'm insane for thinking that, but I just don't get why these kinds of things aren't more widely talked about. It's so neat to think about the potential evolution of society if we decided to approach these kinds of things just as we do with any other scientific research. We would learn so much, and I think it would truly make all of our lives more enticing.

-Submitted by anonymous

Report #2

Hey there, the name is Donny, and I had a frightening encounter while I was with my family in Sun City, Idaho. It happened about fourteen years ago, so I was thirteen years old at the time.

My mom had this friend that she grew up, and they've always stayed in close touch. The woman's name is Linda, and she lived with her daughter and two sons in Sun City. The reason we went out there one summer was that Linda's dad had recently passed away, and that was the last member of her family she had left aside from her kids. My mom knew she was incredibly close to her dad, so she wanted to visit her to provide some support. My dad had to stay behind due to his demanding work schedule, but she pressured me into coming with her. I ended up being glad I did, because Linda's daughter, Kirsten, was a smoke show, and she was less than a year older than me.

Aside from the horror that took place, this was one of the more embarrassing times in my life. I kept doing all these silly things, hoping that Kirsten would notice what a big, strong dude I was. Unfortunately, I was nothing more than a prepubescent, frail pipsqueak. It's one of those things where

I look back and can't help but cringe, especially when I think about what that girl must have genuinely thought about me.

There was this one night amid the week-long vacation that we were all walking along a local trail after sundown. Linda and her kids told us how they had seen many strange things while walking that path. I forgot what they called it, but I remember it was a loop that was probably about four miles from beginning to end. We walked it once during the daytime and didn't see anything peculiar. But I do remember thinking how creepy the place must be once it was dark. That hunch ended up being correct. It was a damn good thing that all of us were together; otherwise, I don't think I would have had the guts to continue onward. I felt a strange presence right after I stepped foot in that forest. Still, I'm pretty sure I cut to the front of the line so that I could prove to Kirsten how courageous I was. By the way, I just cringed as I typed that previous sentence.

I can't remember how long our group had been walking for, but because I was at the front of the line, I was the first to spot it. It looked as if a cloaked figure had risen from a kneeling position, and it grew in size until it was towering over all of us. It stood on a boulder to the right side of the trail, and the first thing that comes to mind when I think about it was how long and skinny its arms were. You're probably inclined to believe that it was just some neighbor or family friend that was playing a cruel joke on us, but there's just no way. The things that this cloaked figure did were beyond the capabilities of a human. Everyone in our group saw it and started screaming hysterically, including the adults. When everyone turned around and started running, I deeply regretted trying to show off by being at the front. It wasn't long after we spotted the figure that I spotted it gliding through the woods off to my left. Soon after that, Kirsten spotted it as well.

"Oh my god, it's chasing us!" she yelled. Maybe those weren't her exact words, but it was something along those lines. The way the figure moved through the forest would have been impossible for any human; it was much too graceful and seemingly effortless. That was the point where I did another incredibly embarrassing thing. After noticing that Kirsten was only a couple of heads in front of me, I weaved around them so that I could get close to her. I then grabbed ahold of her hand and told her something lame about how she shouldn't worry because I was there to protect her. My self-esteem plummeted when she immediately ripped her hand away. I had hoped that this was a rare opportunity for us to grow closer, like what you see in movies, but it was evident she wasn't feeling that. That was when I learned that she wanted nothing to do with me. Looking back at it, I can't blame her; I was an obnoxious little runt. I'm not exactly sure when the cloaked spirit stopped trailing us, but it was when we made it out of the woods that I realized I had been so distracted by my feelings of rejection.

Even though the sighting would have been far too advanced to fabricate, there was a part of me that kept thinking one of the adults would reveal that they had pranked us. That never happened; in fact, everyone was too scared to go back outside, so we had to cancel our plans of toasting marshmallows. It quickly became apparent that Kirsten felt too awkward to look me in the eyes, and I'm not sure she ever acknowledged me for the duration of our trip, which was no more than a day or two.

I'm much older now and have since filled out. I've had a variety of girlfriends that all guys would vote more attractive than Kirsten. Isn't it funny how life works that way? Still, reflecting on how I acted that night makes me feel awkward as hell! Anyway, I don't know what else it was that we could have seen that night other than a ghost. My mom and I have talked about the sighting many times, and she's not at all shy to talk about it with other people. I've noticed that she's good at discussing it in a way that doesn't deter non-believers. Everyone who knows her has always perceived her as an intelligent, respectable individual, so they probably trust that she dealt with something out of the ordinary.

That event is something I think about often, and I would love to learn the full details of what it was that we encountered that night.

-Submitted by Don P.

Report #3

Hi, my name is John, and my experience with the paranormal is something that I'm still trying to accept. Even if they don't outright say it, most people I've told my story to look at me like I'm wacky. But I'll never back down; what I saw was as real as could be, and nobody will ever convince me otherwise. The following incident took place less than four years ago.

When I was in my early twenties, I went my mom to Madison, Wisconsin, to figure out what to do with my grandma's house. My grandma, who my siblings and I referred to as "Nana", had recently passed away, and my mom was going through a very turbulent time. The two of them were extremely close; they'd talk on the phone regularly, so I could only imagine the extent of how my mom felt.

Shortly after we arrived at Nana's house, my mom began crying and talking about how she didn't get a chance to say goodbye. I tried to comfort her by mentioning how that was such a common thing among deaths. I remember asking her whether she would have rather seen Nana hooked up to some machine, which made her barely conscious, just so that she could say goodbye. That's usually the only way people feel like they got some sense of closure before their loved ones make the transition. I tried to tell her that it was a blessing that Nana died peacefully in her sleep, but it seemed as though there was nothing that I could say to comfort her. Both my brother and my sister were texting me, telling me that they had similar experiences. None of us had ever seen Mom that distraught, and her state rapidly worsened while we were inside that house.

My mom asked me if I'd be willing to keep her company while a medium dropped by the house the following day. I'm not going to lie; I've always been terrified by the idea of ghosts, and my mom knew that, but it was apparent she hoped that I'd be able to acquire a bit of courage. I felt that I had no choice other than to give in to her request. I had so much trouble sleeping that night because I imagined what seemed like an endless variety of horrifying scenarios. What if the medium *was* legit but accidentally summoned some malicious spirits while trying to call upon my deceased grandmother? I remember so desperately hoping that this individual was nothing more than a mere con artist, but that they'd at least put on a good show so that my mom could feel more at peace.

When the medium arrived on time the next day, I was surprised to see that it was a man, and a younger one at that; the complete opposite of what I had expected. Sorry if that's sexist, but it's just the truth. The man was probably in his late thirties and preferred to be called "E", which I believe was short for "Evan". He was a taller, thinner man with a crew haircut and small earrings in both ears. Although I found his appearance to be a little suspicious, he quickly made up for it with his polite demeanor.

The three of us had some tea while we chitchatted in the backyard. E explained how he had been fascinated by the paranormal ever since his childhood. He lived in an old house just outside of Milwaukee, and he knew it was haunted. He grew up with bedroom doors, closet doors, kitchen drawers, etc. flinging open for no visible reason. According to him, that was what helped him get used to the fact that ghosts are real and must be treated with respect. He said that he and his parents would often hear others' footsteps throughout their home, even though they were the only ones who lived there.

I remember sitting there totally in awe as I listened to this man's story. It blew my mind that anyone would be willing to live in a creepy environment like that. E talked about it so casually; to him, not only was it not very intimidating, but he spoke about it as if the topic was akin to studying birds or flowers, or anything else out of the ordinary. Even though it was shocking to listen to him, there was something about how he approached it that was comforting. This guy had many years of experience and had no harm done to him; therefore, what did I have to fear? Well, it wasn't long until I'd find out.

After we finished our tea, the three of us proceeded inside and gathered around the dining room table. E presented a piece of art in the form of a tablecloth and rolled it out onto the table. I have no idea what it was for, but it appeared as though it had been used many, many times. After the man asked for a moment of silence, he closed his eyes and seemed to begin meditating. I got the impression that he was trying to center himself so that he'd be able to focus throughout the session. It was probably about five minutes that went by before he slid his forearms toward the center of the table and extended a hand toward each of us. As he did this, his eyes remained closed. I felt so awkward at the idea of holding his hand but went ahead and did it when Mom nudged me with her eyes.

Another few minutes passed where E would occasionally whisper something to himself, though I could never make out what he was saying. I couldn't even tell if he was speaking English or if he was just making subtle noises with his lips. I kept glancing at my mom, wondering whether she was taking this whole thing seriously. While I was sitting there, waiting for something to happen, I became quite confident the entire thing was some silly show. The idea of this guy or anyone taking advantage of my mom's emotions started to make me feel pretty disgusted. I was moments away from ripping my hand away and telling E to get out when, suddenly, his eyelids flung open.

He was gripping my hand extremely hard, and his eyeballs looked to be rolling deeper and deeper into the back of his head. When I looked over at my mom, I could already tell that even she was now wondering whether it was the best idea to have invited this guy over. I now felt very uneasy; it was that type of feeling you get when you realize you shouldn't have gotten involved in something. The best way to describe it would be to say that it's a combination of fear and guilt. At this point, E's grip was very tight around my hand; it was almost as if he was holding onto us so that he wouldn't fall away into another dimension. I was just opening my mouth to ask him if he was okay when he said, "I'm fine." It was so weird; it was as if he had read my mind. It was right after he said it that he repeated it; only this time, it was in a different voice—one that I recognized. It was Nana's voice.

    E's eyelids had closed, and his grip had noticeably loosened. When I looked over at Mom, I noticed there were already tears in her eyes. "Mom, is that you?" she asked, seemingly in disbelief that this whole thing had actually worked.

"I'm okay," Nana's voice announced via E's lips. There was a long period of silence while we attempted to come to terms with this strange reality.

"I miss you so much, Mom," she said to Nana. "I hope you know how much we all love and miss you." E's eyes remained closed. I was so shocked by all of this that I couldn't decide how to contribute to the conversation.

There was another prolonged period of silence before Nana spoke again. This time, she sounded a little nervous. "This isn't safe," she said.

My mom looked at me from across the table; it was clear she was confused. "What...well, what do you mean?" she asked Nana.

There were another ten or so seconds of silence before Nana said something along the lines of, "this isn't safe, dear, you shouldn't have done this." To me, it sounded like Nana was distracted by something, perhaps even hiding from something.

"Nana?" I asked, following more silence. "Are you still there?"

"Not all spirits are malevolent," she suddenly said. She spoke in a way that reminded me how someone tries to simultaneously talk to someone over the phone and another person standing nearby. It was all very odd, and I don't quite know how to write about it.

But my trepidation suddenly shot through the roof when Nana's voice yelled the word "runnnnn!" It was so awful because it sounded like she was getting strangled and gasping for air.

Things only escalated when E's grip around my hand tightened, and he started screaming in his own voice. When I looked over at him, his earlobes were extending downward, as if something was pulling them toward the ground by his earrings. His body began to convulse like there was a scuffle between multiple entities occurring inside his body. I tried to rip my hand away, but his grip was still too strong.

"Let go of me!" I yelled as I rose from my seat. I wanted to run around the table to help my mom, as she was facing the same struggle. Her facial expression indicated that her hand was in pain.

"Take your hand off of her!" I yelled, now full of rage. By this point, I had my right hand around E's wrist, trying to obtain the leverage that would enable me to set myself free. It was no use; all that seemed to do was make his grip even more powerful. I had such a bad feeling and was so determined to break free at that moment that I might have used a machete if there was one available. It felt as though pure evil had a grip on both my mother and I. E wasn't much bigger than me, but I had never before felt physical strength like this. It was clear that some sort of force was using him as a vessel. For what? I had no idea. All I knew at that point was that getting involved in this type of thing was a *terrible* idea.

It wasn't long before E's earrings extended as far down as they could go, causing his earlobes to sever. The earrings, along with several spurts of blood, fell to the floor. E's mouth then opened as wide as it could go. By this point, it felt like the bones in my fingers were on the verge of snapping.

"Aaahhhhhhhh!" my mom screamed out in agony as a couple of her fingers snapped. That provoked me to begin punching E's face, hoping that his own pain receptors would kick in and prompt him to loosen his grip. As you might have suspected, multiple punches to his head didn't do much good. My mom's upper body was now sprawled across the table as she squirmed around from the intense pain. I then felt no choice but to tackle E, which also caused my mother to slide off her chair and onto the ground. It was only a moment later that, finally, E released his grip. His eyes remained closed as his body slowly rose toward the ceiling. With his back against the ceiling, his limbs were sprawled all the way outward. Without another second of hesitation, I ran over to my injured mother and helped her to her feet. I then escorted her out of the house as quickly as I could. By the time we had made it out onto the front lawn, we could still hear E screaming from inside the house.

"What's happening in there!?" a worried-looking neighbor said from the other side of the fence. He was an older-looking man, and I could tell he wanted to offer his condolences regarding the recent death, but the current commotion was much too alarming.

"Would you mind calling the police?" I asked since there was no chance either of us would reenter that home while all of that chaos was unfolding.

It wasn't long before a couple of squad cars arrived that the screaming ceased. It was so awkward because neither my mom nor I could figure out how to explain her broken fingers without throwing E under the bus. I no longer blamed him; there's no question that it was a malicious spirit that had caused him to do that. Even if I had been skeptical about the guy, the fact that I watched his earrings pulled from his ears by some invisible force was enough evidence of his innocence.

Strangely enough, the officers who had rushed inside the home couldn't find anyone. All they found was the mess, including the earrings and drops of blood on the floor. They said that the backdoors were ajar, but there was nobody to be found. The police speculated that, for whatever reason, the man had fled the property by hopping the fence in the backyard.

We never again saw E or heard from him, and we've always wondered what happened to the guy. We didn't know much about his identity, so we could only provide the authorities with his alleged first name and a description of what he looked like. I like to think that he regained control of himself and ran away from the house as quickly as possible. But there's also a part of me that wonders if he could have gotten sucked into another dimension. I realize that might sound far-fetched, but after seeing what we saw that day, I no longer feel that I have a grip on what's possible and what isn't.

I've always tried to dissuade my mom from dwelling on it because she tends to focus on the part where it sounded like her deceased mother was getting strangled. We've always been too intimidated to again reach out to the spirit world, so we've had no way of potentially checking on Nana. The thought that our actions might have somehow opened her up to harm sure does evoke some heavy stress. All we can do at this point is to pray that she's okay.

If you ever find yourself considering whether you should attempt to summon the dead, I highly recommend that you also consider the possible dangers. I have to admit that it feels great to have put all this stuff down on paper. People aren't exaggerating when they mention how therapeutic it can be. It made a much larger impact than I ever could have imagined. If you've dealt with this kind of phenomenon, I urge you to share your recount with Mr. Lyons.

-Submitted by John R.

Report #4

My name is Dale, and I'm close friends with a guy who purchased an old building in Columbus, Ohio, so that he could turn it into a pub. Well, he only ended up being able to acquire the funds to convert the bottom floor. The other two stories have been left untouched, and it's been over eight years since he bought the joint.

The owner's name is Ben, and we grew up together in a suburb of Columbus. We both played football, and it was those two-a-day practices that brought us and some other guys close together. I remember feeling excited for Ben when he finally obtained the building. He had been trying to get it for quite a while, but there was a whole list of obstacles, mostly ones that revolved around acquiring the business license, liquor license, and other bureaucratic nightmares. I've never dealt with anything like that, but from what I've been told, it sucks. I feel bad for the hardworking people who have to go through those mounds of paperwork.

What was interesting about this building was how the third floor was an old ballroom. I've been up there a few times, and the place is magnificent. Ben kept saying he intends to restore the room, but it would undoubtedly cost a fortune. The room is massive and requires all sorts of work; I wouldn't have any clue how to begin with something like that. But aside from the cost, there have been various happenings to keep Ben from frequently visiting the third floor. Frankly, the only reason he even goes to the second floor is that he needed to use the space for extra storage.

I remember the first time I went to the pub to get a beer. It was only a few days before the grand opening, and I think Ben invited about five people, including me. It wasn't long after we all got there that Ben began to talk about the loud footsteps that he had heard from up on that third floor. To him, there was no question that it was ghosts from the past, dancing about the wooden floor. He claimed he had already heard it many times but didn't want to make a fuss about it because he was so busy getting the place ready for business.

His story got even stranger when he mentioned how he had peaked underneath one of the doors from the top of the nearest staircase and saw the bottoms of fancy shoes moving all over the floor. He was about to push the door open so he could see it all, but his instincts warned him that he better not. It was as he was quietly walking back down the staircase that he heard a loud screech coming from the ballroom, and after that, all went silent. Understandably, that prompted him to pick up the pace as he headed back toward the first floor. He had a couple of independent contractors assisting him at the time, and he asked them if they had heard anything strange since they had started coming to the place. Ben said the guys didn't hold back. One of them claimed that they had heard someone running up the steps behind them, screaming, but there was nobody there when he turned around. Also, I think it was the other guy who claimed he had seen a woman walk by an open doorway, but it was from across the ballroom, so he didn't get a good look at her. When he walked over to see who she was and what she was doing there, he couldn't find anyone. It probably had something to do with the fact that they were grown, blue-collar men, that they were reluctant to allow themselves to feel too frightened. But there was one day where one of them didn't show up to work. When Ben called the guy to ask him why he wasn't there, the guy said he woke up with scratches all over his chest. He didn't remember receiving the wounds, but he explained how he felt someone push him from behind while washing his hands at the sink only a day earlier. He said he got a really bad feeling that he shouldn't be there and then waking up with the scratch on his chest affirmed that his intuition was right. He said he didn't even want to call Ben to tell him because he thought it would be safer to cut all ties. But he felt bad when he saw Ben calling and decided to pick up the call at the last second to explain why he wouldn't be coming to work.

Even though the other worker had experienced a few oddities by that point, he still wasn't scared enough to give up the job. From what I understand, he stuck around until Ben no longer needed his services.

As far as my own experiences go, there was only one mild incident where I was at the pub while Ben was closing up for the night. Aside from me, only Ben and one other guy were still there, and both of them were behind the bar. Out of nowhere, it sounded like one of the bathroom stall doors got slammed over and over again, probably about four or five times. The three of us were worried that some drunken idiot got left in there and started vandalizing the place, so we rushed in to stop him. There was nobody in there when we opened the restroom door, but the stall door was hanging from the top hinge. Though puzzled, it was evident that Ben had grown somewhat used to these occurrences and knew that they would continue. I had a feeling that he was forcing himself to accept it as the "new normal". There were early signs that his business would do quite well, and he wasn't about to throw that opportunity away because of paranormal activity. I must admit that his attitude impressed me, as I'm not overly confident that I would have been able to hold it together, had I been in Ben's position.

I think it was a few months after that bathroom incident, right around the start of the holidays, that the strands of Christmas lights were suddenly ripped from the space between the ceiling and the wall. Several strands had been connected and extended around the room from one side of the front door to the next. Just like with the bathroom incident, this one occurred after the pub had closed for the night.

I remember it got to the point where he seemed more reluctant to discuss all those paranormal occurrences. Although he never outright explained why, it might have been because he wanted to suppress the rumors that could prevent customers from wondering whether it might be dangerous to go there.

I stopped drinking a few years back, so I only visit the pub once in a while for an early bite. I do miss the late-night gang, but I just worry I'd be too tempted to have a cocktail. I wonder how much haunted history there is in the small city of Columbus. This kind of stuff makes me wonder about how much if it is happening regularly. If that one building was *that* rich with paranormal occurrences, can you even begin to imagine what happens around the globe every day?

-Submitted by Dale M.

GHOST FRIGHTENING ENCOUNTERS: VOLUME 3

Are you enjoying the read?

I have decided to give back to the readers by making the following eBook **FREE**!

To claim your free eBook, head over to

www.LivingAmongBigfoot.com

and click the "FREE BOOK" tab!

Report #5

Do you ever wonder why humans seem to possess a natural fear of the dark? My hunch is that our instincts are well-aware that ghosts exist. My name is Emily, and I'd like to thank you for taking the time to read my story.

When I was a little girl, somewhere between the ages of six and eight, I was strolling through the woods with my older sister, Cecilia. We must have been less than a mile away from our new house when we stumbled upon an old, abandoned building. I remember it looking like a giant concrete structure. There were shards of glass and scraps of rusted metal all over the place. It looked like something out of one of those post-apocalyptic movies that we see plenty of in modern times. I remember my sister getting super excited when we first spotted the place. She probably thought it would be the perfect secret place for her and her friends to have a party. But what started as something fun and interesting soon turned intensely frightening.

I remember getting an ominous feeling as I followed Cecilia over to the dilapidated structure. I should mention that I hadn't even seen any horror movies. My parents were very strict about not letting me watch anything that might give me nightmares, so I didn't have a frame of reference to worry about what I might be walking into. Still, it was like there was a voice inside my head that warned me to go back. If I hadn't been with my older sister, I can't imagine that I would have continued onward.

After we stepped through what I assume to have been the front entrance, I distinctly remember spotting more than a few old, rusted fire extinguishers on the floor. They must have been there because a group of people had to put out a fire, or, at least, *attempted* to put one out. There was trash littered all over the floor. I couldn't believe how old some of the stuff looked. There were chip bags and candy bar wrappers that looked like they could be more than fifty years old. I ended up getting so distracted by my fascination with the ancient garbage that I hadn't even noticed Cecilia had disappeared. I couldn't believe she had ventured off on her own and left me.

"Cecilia?" I initially called out softly. After a few attempts with no answer, I got a little wound up and couldn't help but scream her name. All that could be heard was my own echo, seemingly bouncing off every wall within the building. I then thought I heard a strange noise coming from the outside; it sounded like a growl of some kind. It creeped me out so much that I went dashing up the steps near the other side of the lobby. After making it to the second floor, it appeared as though I had made it into another lobby. There were broken windows straight ahead of me, and long, dark hallways to off to my left and my right. I couldn't see anyone or anything around me, yet I still had this strange sense that I was being chased. My instincts told me to hide.

Without further hesitation, I ran into the hallway to my left. The first few doors were locked, but when I found a room that was opened, I dashed into the darkness and hid behind the furthest side of what looked to be an old steel desk. As quiet as possible, I sat there waiting, hoping that it would be any second before I heard my sister's voice. Instead, I soon heard what sounded like two sets of footsteps. It sounded like super heavy boots that had metal buckles all over them. Even though I had no idea who they were, I remember having a powerful feeling that I shouldn't let them find me. It was so weird. It was as if my instincts knew that I was in danger.

After the heavy boots seemingly made their way to the end of the hallway, my brain scrambled as I tried to decide what was best to do. Should I continue to hide? Should I quietly resume my search for my sister? Or should I run out of the place and get home as quickly as possible?

It was maybe about thirty seconds later that I began to rise to my feet but froze as soon as I heard a new set of footsteps hurry into the room. It was so dark, but my eyes had adjusted enough to make out the familiar silhouette. It was Cecilia.

"Oh, thank God you're okay!" my sister whispered as she embraced my shoulders. Her voice was stuttering, and I could tell she was petrified.

"What happened? Who's out there?" I muttered, but she aggressively shoved the tip of her finger against my lips. Clearly, she didn't want whoever was out there to get ahold of us. My sister grabbed my hand and rushed me toward the door. She then leaned against the wall so that she could listen for any activity within the hallway. After she determined that the coast was clear, we raced in the direction that I had come, soon to turn the corner and head down the stairs. As soon as we turned the corner after the first set up steps, we were stopped dead in our tracks. A giant dark figure stood on the staircase.

I was only able to see it for a split-second because my sister instantly jerked me around and ran me back up the steps. That image of that figure still haunts me to this day. It was a tall, wide-shoulder man with all black clothing and a grey face. His head tilted in such a strange way as soon as he spotted us. The main thing I remember is his eyes. I suppose it could be a fragment of my childhood imagination, but I remember the eyes appearing so lifeless and way too large in proportion to the head.

After running back up the steps and into the hallway that we had only just come from, I tried to tell Cecilia to stop. I was convinced we were headed straight for the others who were walking around with the heavy boots. I couldn't see them when I was hiding, but it was easy to hear that they were headed in the same direction that we were now running. It might have been because I wasn't articulating it well enough, but Cecilia wouldn't hear it. She just kept telling me to hush as we made our way down the long, dimly lit hallway. As I ran, I distinctly remember trying to keep my eyes on the floor because I didn't want to see another one of whatever that was that we had just encountered on the staircase.

Eventually, we ended up at another set of steps, and when we turned the corner on that one, I expected to spot another one of those strange men. Fortunately, it was clear. Across the hall at the end of the staircase was a pair of doors. We were able to push our way through one of them, and I can't even begin to emphasize just how happy I was to get out of that building. After sprinting around the outside of the building, my sister spotted the path we used to get there. When we made it into the woods, we felt we were far enough away and could take a brief moment to catch our breath. That was when we turned around and saw the creepiest site yet. There had to have been five or six of those strange men. They all looked similar, and they appeared to be floating around near the doorway we used. It was clear they could see us. We didn't spend a whole lot of time examining the strange men; it was probably only a couple of seconds before my sister again grabbed my hand and yanked me deeper into the trail.

When we made it home, she told my parents all about what we had just come across. Even though most of it must have been hard for my parents to believe, they could tell we had been genuinely frightened by something, so they called the police to ask them to check things out. I specifically remember the police asking my mom to ask us whether the strangers had touched us in any way. We said no. Still, it was more than understandable that my parents didn't like the idea of shady men hanging out at an abandoned building near our home. And there was something incredibly creepy about it, given that the structure was so secluded.

It wasn't very long before the police called back and informed us that, although they found the building, they couldn't find any trace of anyone. It's probably worth noting that neither of us had seen any cars near the facility. How would those strange men have gotten there without vehicles? We both thought they looked to be soldiers of some kind;

however, they didn't look like soldiers from modern times. Their outfits looked like they could have been from the 1940s. But that face we saw on the staircase didn't look quite human. I'd even go as far as to say it looked sort of demonic. And, of course, the way they appeared to be hovering outside the building was the strangest aspect of the day. After Tom Lyons read my report for the first time, he asked me to submit my best guest about what we encountered. Reading the first issue of *Ghost Frightening Encounters* was what made me confident that we had run into a group of ghosts.

Not only did that whole experience scare me away from ever wanting to wander too far into the woods again, but it also made it so I couldn't tolerate supernatural horror films. Years ago, one of my ex-boyfriends tried to get me to watch one, and I nearly had a panic attack. I tried to explain why I was so terrified of that sort of thing, but I think he concluded I was a little bit crazy. I can't necessarily blame him; after all, I sometimes have trouble believing that all of that happened, but I assure you it did.

    I sure do appreciate being able to share my supernatural experience. I think it's such a good thing that these types of books are out there; it's comforting to know that you're not alone.

-Submitted by Emily C.

Report #6

My name is Joseph, and it was back when I was a toddler that I would see specters in the basement of my old house in Waukegan, Illinois. I often wonder why I didn't seem all that bothered by them. I'm much more intimidated by the idea in my adult years. Strange how things work that way. Therefore, my question is: do we possess a natural fear of ghosts, or do we develop the fear as we become older and more cynical?

There was this one Christmas where I received what was probably my favorite childhood toy. It was a little roller coaster made of plastic. It wasn't anything complicated; it was pretty much just an oval-shaped set of train tracks that had shallow slopes. When I think about it now, the toy seems kind of lame, but I sure did have a blast playing on it. I mention that toy because, even though my memory is vague, I'm sure it was while I was playing with that toy that I saw one the visitors for the first time. My parents perceived that basement to be a pretty safe place, so they weren't afraid to leave me alone for little bits of time while they tended to tasks. I remember the carpet was excessively soft, so there was no way I could fall and hurt myself.

I remember I was coming around the bend at one end of the tracks when I noticed a woman in the room near the opposite side. She was sitting on the floor in a deranged position. All these years later, I'm still not sure how to describe it. The closest thing I can compare it to are those yoga people who can bend their limbs into all sorts of shapes. Sometimes it feels like I'm about to pull a muscle just thinking about it. When you're a small child, it seems like you're often in a dreamlike state. What I mean by that is that you tend to go with the flow in many more ways than you do when you mature. Many things don't make sense, but you carry on not caring or developing perceptions that are rarely logical. At this point in my life, I don't believe I had considered what ghosts are, and I don't know if I would go as far as to say I was frightened of this woman who had appeared in the room, but I do somewhat remember my intuition warning me not to make her upset.

I remained aboard the little toy cart as I approached her. She didn't look angry or anything; she just had this sort of soft, empty stare. As I got close to her, I remember seeing the cloudiness in her eyes. When I was only a few feet away, one of my parents came back into the room, but the mysterious woman disappeared before they could notice her. I'm not sure whether I even mentioned the woman to my parents that first time. If I had, they disregarded the idea as part of my imagination.

It was probably within the next couple of days that I was once again riding the roller coaster by myself when another stranger appeared in the room. This one was wearing, what I thought at the time, was a hooded sweatshirt. But looking back at it, I now believe it was a cloak. I remember it looking a lot like what the grim reaper is often depicted to be wearing, only it was brown instead of the usual black. They paced back and forth near a section of the wall that was near the doorway. From what I recall, they didn't seem to pay any attention to me, and I didn't do anything to try to get them to acknowledge me. I wasn't able to see that particular visitor's face, so, for all I know, it could have been the same woman that I had seen before. The only reason I'm not certain is that there were *others* who would soon visit.

Because I was so young when all of this started, I don't know how long it went on. I'm not even sure whether it continued for the entire duration my family lived in that house. All I remember is that I got used to these strangers randomly appearing while I was in that basement.

There was this other time when I wasn't riding the train, but I was sitting on the floor and coloring or looking at some book when I felt a presence behind me. I turned around to find a man looking over my shoulder, seemingly observing what I was doing. Just like the others, the man didn't say anything. I think he disappeared soon after.

It seemed like there were countless occasions similar to the ones I just mentioned. Although I don't think I saw it this way at the time, the most frightening one of all was when the strange lady appeared in the center of the toy roller coaster tracks. She was lying on her back and appeared to be shaking uncontrollably. I don't recall her making any noise, and I didn't even perceive it to be any kind of violent image at the time. I suppose my brain wasn't yet developed enough to associate the scene with darkness. As far as I can remember, she never approached me.

I once went to see an alleged supernatural "expert" who worked at a local crystal shop, hoping that they'd be able to provide me with some new insight. Unfortunately, it ended up being a speculation session and a monumental waste of money.

I've told a few people I'm close to about those occurrences, and they almost always try to convince me that they couldn't be anything more than mere childhood delusions. I completely get where those people are coming from, but it's still frustrating. Yes, I was very young, but I know it happened. I've never seen a sasquatch or an alien, but it's because of what I experienced that I give those reports the benefit of the doubt. It's a shame that society can't work together to uncover the truth.

-Submitted by Joseph G.

GHOST FRIGHTENING ENCOUNTERS: VOLUME 3

Report #7

It was 2009 when I was with my college boyfriend at a remote place that was maybe five miles from our campus. We went to school in Indiana, and there was a ton of farmland around us. It felt so incredibly desolate at nighttime, which made it spooky but also romantic. There would be times when we would sit in the car, sipping from a flask or whatever, and I was convinced I would see movement behind the wood line. Still, it was never enough to clarify that there was anyone else out there with us. But even with that romantic, eerie atmosphere, I never in a million years would have suspected to see what we did on one autumn night.

My boyfriend's name was Brian. He was a typical frat boy that loved to party and did the bare-minimum, academically. He was funny because he was always so good around professors and my parents. He could win anyone over with ease. It probably had something to do with that great smile of his. It was intoxicating. And it would be that same smile that convinced me to go camping with him one weekend night in early autumn soon after we got back from summer break.

I had a bad feeling as soon as we parked the car. Something made me not want to get out. But, once again, Brian was able to persuade me. I remember how he started walking into the trail without me, and the last thing I wanted was to be left alone. I didn't even understand where exactly we were; all I knew was that we parked at a spot we had never gone to before.

Brian had a small speaker hanging from his backpack that was playing music. Although it helped to lighten the mood, it didn't enable us to hear whether any people or animals approached us. I got annoyed with Brian because he brought the tiniest flashlight, and he didn't even have any backup batteries. He was a fun guy, but that was a great example of how he could sometimes be very reckless. He just kept insisting that everything was going to be just fine. Had I had even the slightest idea of what would happen that night, I would have refused to continue onward.

It was probably only about a half of a mile walk to the campsite, but it felt a lot longer than that because of how I was growing more nervous by the second. By the time we had arrived, Brian was already drunk. I guess I was so focused on checking our surroundings that I hadn't noticed he had been sipping his flask during the hike. It was my first time setting up a tent, so I wasn't very much help. As Brian was securing the rain guard to the top of the tent, we heard rustling from somewhere behind him. It sounded like two feet running a bunch of leaves. Brian shined that tiny flashlight of his at the trees behind him. At first, neither of us spotted anything other than thin branches blowing in the breeze.

"Must have been a deer," Brian said before resuming setting up the tent.

"Deer don't walk on two legs," I said, somewhat irritated by the stupidity of his comment.

Only a few moments later, we heard the same noise, not too far off from where we heard it the last time. Once again, Brian spun around and aimed the flashlight near the woods. We got the tiniest glimpse of what looked like a child running behind one of the larger trees. Why would a child be all the way out there, unaccompanied? It made absolutely zero sense. We were nowhere near anyone's house. Brian whispered how he thought we were at least a mile away from any residences.

"Excuse me?" Brian said, in a confused but gentle tone. "Is anyone out there? Do you need help?"

There was no answer. It happened so quickly that neither of us managed to see whether it was a little boy or a little girl. Brian called out to the child again, but there was still no response. We weren't about to let some small child hangout near our campsite, so Brian walked over to the tree to find them. I watched him peak his head around the trunk, but it quickly became apparent that he didn't see anyone. I remember him shining his light upward, thinking that the kid might have somehow scurried up the tree, but no luck there either. It was when he had made his way over to me that we heard the footsteps once again; only this time, they had come from the opposite side of us.

By this point, I was genuinely scared. It felt like there was a lot of tension in the air, and I somehow knew it wasn't just coming from my fear; it felt different. Also, it suddenly got a lot colder. And I mean it when I say *a lot*. It was unlike any sensation I had ever felt.

"I want to go," I said to Brian, but it was like he didn't hear me. He seemed way more focused on shining his light toward the wood line, wanting to expose whatever was out there. I walked over to him and stood behind him, and it was as I had turned my gaze just a little bit to my left that I noticed the figure behind me. I couldn't help but scream as I saw the little boy. I saw him for only a brief second before he ran off in the opposite direction, but he looked sick. Also, he wasn't wearing modern clothing; he appeared as though he had come straight out of the 1930s or even 1920s.

I had accidentally screamed so loud in Brian's ear that it caused him to fumble the flashlight, and it fell to the ground and broke. The realization that our only source of light was gone manifested the most dreadful feelings yet. I'm not sure why, because we hadn't seen or heard anything of the sort, but losing that light suddenly made it feel as though monsters surrounded us, and that they wouldn't hesitate to close in on us. The more I think about it, the more I realize that this was the kind of energy that this mysterious little boy brought to the table. It was as if his presence had a way of altering the ambiance, converting the environment into something straight out of a nightmare. By this point, I didn't even need to demand that we leave; Brian was more than determined to make it back to the vehicle.

I'm not even sure whether we cared enough to grab the entirety of our belongings before we began the trek. As we heard little footsteps in the woods alongside us, I remember thinking I would have done anything to reverse time and never agree to go out there.

"Ow! What the hell!?" Brian suddenly called out while as he stopped to wince. He claimed that he felt a stone or something hit his hipbone. That freaked me out so badly that I couldn't help but start running. I could barely see the path in front of me, but I didn't care; All I could think about was getting away from the mischievous little boy that now seemed interested in harming us.

"Ahh!" Brian winced again from behind me as another stone hit him. That prompted me to speed up, which led to me tripping and scraping my knee pretty badly. Before I knew it, Brian helped me to my feet, and we were soon running alongside one another. There was one instance where it sounded as though heavier footsteps were coming after us, as though a man rather than a boy was following us. We were too focused on not tripping along the path to turn around to look at who was following us. To this day, I don't think I've ever been more relieved than when we finally spotted Brian's car.

While we were driving away, I braced myself because I anticipated that another stone might get whipped at one of the windows, but it never happened. Neither of us even saw anyone outside while we were heading toward the road. It almost seemed like someone just wanted to chase us away from that area for whatever reason.

When we made it back to Brian's dorm, we quickly learned that his wounds from the stones were very real—seeing those welts made the whole experience sink in even more than before. There was something about seeing those marks that made everything even more unsettling.

I suppose there is the slim chance that there could have been a living child out there, but I find it very hard to believe that any kid would have wanted to be out in that area at that time and without a flashlight. That just wouldn't make any sense. And even if that was the case, why would they want to hurt us?

Please be cautious when going into isolated areas. If I hadn't been with Brian, I don't know what might have happened. I might very well have ended up being one of those people who mysteriously disappears in the woods.

-Submitted by anonymous

Report #8 (Steve Molloy's Report Continued)

What did this mean? Why would Bobby have written "under the frog statue" on my bathroom mirror? I contemplated disregarding it as a figment of my imagination, but I couldn't; the words were clear. It didn't take me very long to guess what he was referring to because I knew quite well of the goofy decoration that stood in front of the koi pond in the front yard of the house Bobby grew up in. I say it looked goofy because it didn't at all match the rest of the yard's aesthetic. The property looked like something straight out of the English countryside. The mansion had aged ivy growing all over the front, and there was a large pool in the backyard that resembled something that belonged to the Great Gatsby. But that frog statue was something that all of Bobby's friends commented on. Basically, it was a frog's head on a man's body. It was dressed in a fancy suit with a bowtie and leaned on a cane.

Many people would perceive Bobby's family as somewhat posh, and something about that statue just didn't match. I was deeply puzzled as to why Bobby would have mentioned that thing, but I couldn't come up with any other reason other than that he wanted me to look underneath it.

Nothing strange occurred during the remainder of that night, but I was far too shaken to fall back asleep. I kept contemplating whether I should head over to the house and ask if I could check underneath the statue. If I did decide to go through with the strange task, would it be better if I asked Bobby's mother, or should I climb over the fence and take care of it in the middle of the night while everyone at the house was asleep? The only reason I was even considering trespassing is that I had no idea how I would even begin to explain to Bobby's mom or anyone who still lived there about what I was doing.

The next day, I couldn't stop thinking about the whole thing. It was such a nagging feeling that disabled me from concentrating on routine tasks. I desperately wanted the entire thing to have been nothing more than a strange dream, but I knew it wasn't. It quickly became apparent that I couldn't return to a remotely regular routine until I pursued the mystery. Bobby was such a good guy and meant so much to me; I could tell it was going to eat away at me if I didn't at least attempt to explore why his spirit would have written those words on my bathroom mirror.

I'm still not positive whether it was the best way to go about things, but I ended up asking Bobby's mother if it would be okay with her if I just walked around the yard for a bit and reflected on all the good times I had had with her son. I guess she took it as a heartwarming sentiment because she immediately got teary-eyed and hugged me on her front doorstep. Feeling it was too hard to talk anymore, she waved me off to do as I pleased before closing the door behind her.

I played it cool and casually strolled to the side of the house. I didn't want it to look like I had any specific mission in mind, in case someone was watching me from inside, so I spent a bit of time admiring the sky and the flowers. I wanted to appear as though I was merely breathing in the air and engaged in deep thought.

When it felt like enough time had passed, I veered toward the koi pond and sat down on the nearby stone bench. After around five to ten minutes had gone by, I began to get anxious. I checked over my shoulder to make sure that I couldn't see anyone, and then walked a few steps over to the frog statue. It was as soon as I tilted it onto its side that I could tell the soil beneath it had been tampered with. I didn't have to dig very deep at all before I discovered a cigar box and a handgun. I got an awful feeling as soon as I spotted the firearm, but I was confident that there was a good reason why Bobby had led me to find it. Within the cigar box was a blank card with a pleasant painting of a rose garden on the front. I only needed to skim over it before I realized it was a suicide note, written by Bobby's youngest brother. I staggered to stand up. It felt like I had lost my breath.

I didn't know what else to do other than walk back over to the front door and hand the note to Bobby's mother. It was the last thing I wanted her to see, but if I hadn't shown it to someone who would immediately intervene, how long would it be until she ended up with another dead child? I had to choose the lesser of two very grim outcomes. When she asked where I found it, I told her what I think to be a white lie. I explained that the frog statue appeared to be leaning slightly to the right, so I walked over to adjust it, and that was when I felt a solid object poking out of the soil. That was when I told her that the gun was still over there. I didn't think it was necessary to tell her about the paranormal events that had taken place in my car and at my home. I just couldn't imagine it bringing her any comfort. She quickly called the police to come over and take the firearm away. Bobby's brother wasn't home at that time, but fortunately, he returned home to professionals who were able to intervene and get him to reconsider suicide. Honestly, even the thought that I might have disregarded those words on the bathroom mirror is enough to give me the chills.

I've never met anyone who has experienced anything comparable to my story, but I know they must be out there. Trust me—paranormal happenings occur all the time. If you've ever thought you might have seen a ghost, there's a darn good chance you did.

-Submitted by Steve Molloy

GHOST FRIGHTENING ENCOUNTERS: VOLUME 3

Conclusion

Thanks for reading *GHOST FRIGHTENING ENCOUNTERS*. If you're looking for something else to sink your teeth into, you'll love *WENDIGO WOODS*. It's a thrilling true story!

GHOST FRIGHTENING ENCOUNTERS: VOLUME 3

Editor's Note

Before you go, I'd very much like to say "thank you" for purchasing this book.

I'm aware you had an endless variety of paranormal books to choose from, but you took a chance on my content. Therefore, thanks for reading this one and sticking with it to the last page.

At this point, I'd like to ask you for a *tiny* favor; it would mean the world to me if you could leave a review where you purchased this book.

Your feedback will aid me as I continue to create products that you and many others will enjoy.

GHOST FRIGHTENING ENCOUNTERS: VOLUME 3

GHOST FRIGHTENING ENCOUNTERS: VOLUME 3

Mailing List Sign Up Form

Don't forget to sign up for the newsletter email list. I promise this will not be used to spam you, but only to ensure that you will always receive the first word on any new releases, discounts, or giveaways! All you need to do is simply click the following URL and enter your email address.

URL-

http://eepurl.com/dhnspT

GHOST FRIGHTENING ENCOUNTERS: VOLUME 3

Social Media

Feel free to follow/reach out to me with any questions or concerns on either Instagram or Twitter! I will do my best to follow back and respond to all comments.

Instagram:
@living_among_bigfoot

Twitter:
@AmongBigfoot

GHOST FRIGHTENING ENCOUNTERS: VOLUME 3

About the Editor

A simple man at heart, Tom Lyons lived an ordinary existence for his first 52 years. Native to the great state of Wisconsin, he went through the motions of everyday life, residing near his family and developing a successful online business. The world that he once knew would completely change shortly after moving out west, where he was confronted by the allegedly mythical species known as Bigfoot.

You can email him directly at:

Living.Among.Bigfoot@gmail.com

Printed in Great Britain
by Amazon